Published by OH!
20 Mortimer Street
London W1T 3JW

ISBN 978-1-80069-008-0

Compiled by: Theresa Bebbington
Editorial: Lisa Dyer
Project manager: Russell Porter
Design: Tony Seddon
Production: Freencky Portas

A CIP catalogue record for this book is available from the British Library

Printed in Dubai

10 9 8 7 6 5 4 3 2 1

THE LITTLE BOOK OF

# TREES

AN ARBORETUM OF TREE LORE

# CONTENTS

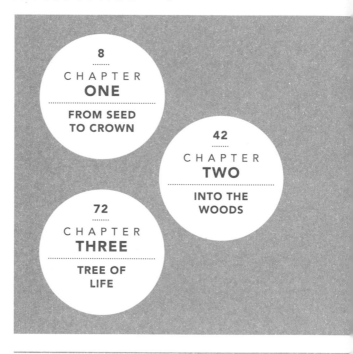

# INTRODUCTION

You don't need to be a tree hugger to love trees. Trees have been living on our planet for almost 400 million years, providing shelter, food and shade to wildlife, as well as being "carbon sinks" – storing the carbon dioxide they absorb – and expelling oxygen that we need for breathing. Whether they grow in cities or form part of a huge rainforest, trees are essential to the life and wellbeing of ourselves and our planet. Here you will learn why we need them and how we've lived alongside them throughout the centuries. You'll find snippets of information on trees, inspirational quotes and proverbs, and learn about tree superstitions and customs from different countries.

In the first chapter "From Seed to Crown", you will find fascinating facts about the anatomy of the tree, including one species that grows its fruit on the trunk rather than from its branches, and which are the oldest and tallest trees in the world. "Into the Woods" takes a look at woods, forests and rainforests, and the relationships between trees, such as how they send out signals to alert other trees of danger. "Tree of Life" explores how wildlife benefits from trees, even ones that are decaying or dead.

The remaining chapters focus on human interaction with trees, starting with "Urban Trees", which explains the benefits of planting trees in city settings, from improving health to preventing flooding. You'll find an eclectic mix of ancient beliefs about trees in "Folklores and Superstitions", such as fairies who grant wishes if you catch a falling leaf. "Customs and Rituals" takes a look at the practices from around the world linked to trees, such as why juniper is burnt in temples.

To complete your knowledge on trees, you'll find lists of favourite song titles and books that mention trees, as well as famous trees in history and glossaries on collective nouns for trees. *The Little Book of Trees* is crammed full of information, history and folklore that will keep any dendrophile turning the pages.

CHAPTER
**ONE**

# From Seed to Crown

**The living tree is presented here in all its magnificence, from its roots in the ground to its canopy of branches and leaves.**

**❝**

*For in the true nature of things, if we rightly consider, every green tree is far more glorious than if it were made of gold or silver.*

**❞**

**Martin Luther**,
German theologian (1483–1546)

# Naked Seeds

Trees that do not flower produce "naked" gymosperm seeds. These include pine cones made of woody scales; on female cones, each scale has an ovule that needs to be fertilized by pollen from a male pine cone to become a seed. Other examples include yew seeds and tiny juniper cones.

# *Fleshy Fruit*

Many trees are angiosperms, meaning their seeds are produced in ovaries within the flower. Examples include the fleshy fruit from apple and pear trees, trees with stone fruit (the seed is inside the stone, such as cherry and plum trees, and trees with berries, such as persimmon and mulberry trees.

# A seed hidden in the heart of an apple is an orchard invisible.

Welsh proverb

# Trunk-sprouting Fruit

Also known as the Brazilian grapetree, the jabuticaba has a unique way of producing fruit – it grows on its trunk! This unusual method makes it easier for animals to reach the fruit, who eat it and then disperse the seeds. The fruit is available all year round on this evergreen tree.

# *Helicopters*

Whether you called them helicopters or twirling birds, most people remember winged seeds from their childhood. A pair of wings extending from the base of the seedpods cause them to spin as they fall from the tree, and wind helps to disperse them. Examples include seeds from maple, hornbeam and ash trees.

# *Nuts*

Angiosperm fruit from some trees have a hard protective husk or shell surrounding their seeds; we call them nuts.

Tree nuts include almonds, Brazil nuts, cashews, chestnuts, hazelnuts, macadamias, pecans, pistachios and walnuts, and, of course, acorns from oak trees.

**66**

*The creation of a thousand forests is in one acorn.*

**99**

**Ralph Waldo Emerson**,
American essayist, poet and philosopher
(1803–1882)

# *Oldest Living Trees*

Bristlecone pine trees are
among the oldest-living organisms on
Earth. Methuselah is one of
the oldest at about

## **4,852 years old.**

Its location is a secret because, in
1964, a doctoral student cut down
another bristlecone, the almost
4,900-year-old Prometheus. An older
bristlecone, at over 5,060 years, was
discovered near Methuselah in 2013.

# *Counting Rings*

Dendrochronology is the science of dating and studying annual growth rings in trees.

But dating a tree by counting rings is only about 40 per cent accurate. The amount of water a tree absorbs alters the width of a growth ring. Rings are wider during rainier years and narrower in dry years.

# Glossary of Tree Anatomy

### Bark:
tough protective outer layer of a tree's trunk, branches and twigs; an inner bark layer passes food to the rest of the tree

### Conifer:
an "evergreen" tree that bears cones

### Crown:
the branches, twigs, buds, leaves, flower and fruit of a tree

### Deciduous:
referring to trees that drop their leaves in autumn

### Fruit:
formed from the tree's flowers,
providing protection for its seeds

### Hardwood:
deciduous, broad-leaved trees
(note that a hardwood can have
soft wood)

### Leaves:
blades on stalks on hardwoods;
needles and scales on conifers

*continued overleaf...*

### Roots:
base of the tree, typically underground,
with smaller fibres that absorb water and
nutrients from the soil and larger branches
that anchor the tree to the ground and
store nitrogen and carbohydrates

### Seed:
produced by the tree to create
a new plant

### Softwood:
needle-leaved trees, usually evergreen

### Tree:
a woody plant with roots, trunk and crown

### Trunk:
the main body of a tree

**"**

*A forest is a living thing
like a human body...
each part dependent on
all the other parts.*

**"**

**Louis L'Amour,**
American novelist (1908–1988)

# *Deep Roots*

Tree roots normally grow in
the top 45 centimetres (18in) of soil.
But some species, such as the bald
cypress, form exposed "knees" when
growing near water, which supply
air to underwater roots. A wild fig
in South Africa's Echo Caves has the
deepest roots, thought to be about

# 122 metres (400ft) deep.

# Though a tree grows so high, the falling leaves return to the root.

Malay proverb

**"**

*A tree has roots in the soil*
*yet reaches to the sky. It tells us*
*that in order to aspire we need to be*
*grounded and that no matter*
*how high we go it is from our roots*
*that we draw sustenance.*

**"**

**Wangari Maathai,**
Kenyan political activist (1940–2011)

**"**

*In a forest of a hundred thousand trees, no two leaves are alike. And no two journeys along the same path are alike.*

**"**

**Paulo Coelho,**
Brazilian novelist (1947– )

# The Living Dead

Only 1 per cent of a mature tree contains living cells.

The remaining 99 per cent of the tree is composed of non-living cells, but they are important for support, transporting water and nutrients, and defence.

Although non-living cells aren't biologically alive, they are only considered dead when detached from the tree.

# *Getting to the Heart of It*

Under a trunk's exterior bark layer
grows the newly formed, light-
coloured, living sapwood, where water
is transported to the leaves.

As the tree grows and new sapwood
is formed, the older sapwood ages,
becomes darker and the cells die
to form the heartwood, the central
support for the tree.

# World's Tallest Trees

A coast redwood tree named
Hyperion is the world's tallest tree
at about

# 116 metres (380ft).

To prevent damage to the tree, its
location remains a secret.

The Centurion, at almost 101 metres
(331ft), is the world's second-tallest
tree. This eucalyptus tree grows
in Tasmania.

# World's Widest Tree

A Montezuma cypress named Árbol del Tule holds the title of the world's widest tree. It has a circumference of

## 42 metres (138ft)

and diameter of

## 11.6 metres (38ft).

It can be found in the Mexican state of Oaxaca.

# *Predicting Colour*

Check the weather forecast
before deciding when to head
outdoors to catch the changing
colour of autumnal leaves.

Deciduous tree leaves
can turn spectacular shades
of yellow, red, purple and
orange as daylight lessens
and temperatures drop.

Low temperatures above freezing will produce bright reds in maples, however an early frost will weaken them.

Surprisingly, a sunny day doesn't produce the best display: a rainy or overcast day will help to intensify the colours.

A greyish, cool and dry day that's above freezing is the best day to head to the woods.

# Why Do Leaves Change Colour?

With less light and cooler temperatures, leaves can't keep up with their food-making process. This leads to chlorophyll breaking down and their green colour disappearing – and allows yellows and oranges to show through. Other chemical changes occur at the same time, such as the production of anthocyanin pigments, which create reds.

**❝**

*The great trees, which had looked
shrunken and bare in the earlier months,
had now burst into strong life and health;
and stretching forth their green arms over
the thirsty ground, converted open and
naked spots into choice nooks, where was a
deep and pleasant shade from which to look
upon the wide prospect...*

**❞**

**Charles Dickens**,
*Oliver Twist*, 1838

# *Forever Evergreen*

Not all trees lose their leaves in
autumn. Evergreen trees, such
as pines, spruces, firs, hemlocks
and cedars – basically most of the
conifers – have needle-like leaves
that are green all year round. While
they don't drop off altogether,
individual leaves do drop off after
2–4 years or more.

**66**

*It's only in winter
that the pine and cypress
are known
to be evergreen.*

**99**

**Confucius**,
Chinese philosopher (551–479 BC)

CHAPTER
**TWO**

# Into the Woods

**Take a walk through the woods, forests and rainforests that blanket our world, from the arboretum to the Amazon.**

# *Collective Nouns for Trees*

Unlike a shrub or bush, a tree has a single stem
or trunk emerging from the roots. But what
terms are used for a group of trees?

### *Arboretum:*
botanical collection of trees

### *Avenue:*
two rows of trees bordering a way or road

### *Bush:*
shrub; wild, uncultivated land
(Africa and Australia);
indigenous rainforest (New Zealand)

### *Chaparral:*
dense thickets of trees

### *Clearing:*
area in a wood or forest cleared of trees

### *Clump:*
group of trees on a hilltop

### *Coppice:*
area of woodland in which trees are cut
back heavily to encourage growth

### *Copse:*
small area of trees with undergrowth

### *Dell:*
small hollow or valley covered with trees

### *Forest:*
large area of trees

*continued overleaf...*

### Grove:
small group of trees

### Hanger:
small group of trees on the side
of a steep hill

### Krummholz:
stunted trees growing in exposed
areas at high latitude

### Monoculture:
group of trees of only one species

### Orchard:
group of trees managed for
their nuts or fruit

### Plantation:
area of trees planted for
commercial purposes

### *Spinney:*
small area of trees, traditionally
for hunting game

### *Stand:*
area of forest with uniform tree species

### *Thicket:*
dense area of trees

### *Withy:*
group of willows

### *Wood/woodland:*
area of land covered with trees –
smaller than a forest

# A society grows great when old men plant trees in whose shade they know they shall never sit.

Greek proverb

# A–Z of Species

In 2017 a scientific global census established that there were more than 60,000 known tree species, alphabetically starting with *Abarema abbottii*, which is found only in the Dominican Republic, and ending with the rare *Zygophyllum kaschgaricum*, native to China and Kyrgyzstan.

Overall, there are about 3 trillion trees on Earth.

# Young... and Old

Old Tjikko is a Norway spruce, but it can be found in Sweden.

The above ground part of the tree is relatively young, but the roots have been growing for

## 9,550 years.

The Norway spruce can clone itself, so when one tree dies, another one grows up from the same roots.

**“**

*A woodland in full colour
is awesome as a forest fire,
in magnitude at least,
but a single tree is like
a dancing tongue of flame
to warm the heart.*

**”**

**Hal Borland**,
American author and naturalist (1900–1978)

# *Lost in the Woods?*

Trees can help point you in the right
direction. In temperate northern
climates, moss grows on the more
shady northern side of a tree trunk.
Tree rings, if you can see them, will
be thicker on the southern side,
which gets more sunlight.
The opposite is true in the
Southern Hemisphere.

**"**

*The trees encountered
on a country stroll*

*Reveal a lot about the
country's soul...*

*A culture is no better
than its woods.*

**"**

**W. H. Auden**,
English poet (1907–1973)

# Forests of Different Ages

Not all forests are the same – they can be classed by how established they are.

*Young, open forests,* with shrubs, grasses and young trees, are created by logging and fire. In North America, black bears, goldfinches and bluebirds are attracted to this type of environment.

### *Middle-aged forests*
have taller trees that outgrow
weaker vegetation and trees.
Their open canopy is perfect for
ground vegetation, which attracts
salamanders, elk and tree frogs.

### *Old forests*
have a complex canopy formed
by large trees, as well as a
well-developed understorey
of vegetation that hosts bats,
squirrels, birds and many
other animals.

**"**

*It is not so much for its beauty
that the forest makes a claim upon
men's hearts, as for that subtle
something, that quality of air that
emanation from old trees,
that so wonderfully changes and
renews a weary spirit.*

**"**

**Robert Louis Stevenson**,
Scottish novelist (1850–1894)

# *Strangler Tree*

In Australia, a bird, bat or other
animal carries the sticky seed of a
strangler fig to a high branch of a
tree. From here, a seed grows roots
down the trunk of the host tree until
they take root in the ground. The
roots graft together and enclose
the host tree.

# *Cedars of God*

About 400 survivors remain from the Cedars of God forest in Lebanon. Once an extensive forest, it is mentioned in the Bible more than 70 times. Resin from the trees was used for mummification in ancient Egypt, and the trees were used to construct the First Temple of Jerusalem in King Solomon's time.

# World's Oldest Forests

***Daintree Rainforest:*** Australia,
100–180 million years old

***Borneo Lowland Rainforest:*** Indonesia,
130–140 million years old

***Taman Negara:*** Malaysia, 130 years old

***The Amazon Rainforest:*** South America,
55 million years old

***Réunion National Park Forest:***
Madagascar, 2–2.5 million years old

***Kakamega Forest:*** Kenya,
over 2 million years old

# Underground Network

Trees share a symbiotic relationship with mycorrhizal fungi. The fungi live on the tree's roots and help them absorb water; the trees in turn provide them with sugars.

But what's really amazing about this relationship is that it works on a much larger underground scale that connects entire forests.

The fungi link older, large "mother" trees to tens of dozens of smaller nearby trees.

Mother trees can send extra carbon to seedlings using the mycorrhizal network, which can increase seedling survival rate by four times.

CHAPTER
**THREE**

# Tree of Life

**Essential for the survival of wildlife and humans, trees provide protection and sustenance to all within their vital ecosystem.**

# Around a flowering tree, one finds many insects.

Guinea proverb

**66**

*Ancient trees are precious.
There is little else on Earth that plays
host to such a rich community of life
within a single living organism.*

**99**

**Sir David Attenborough**,
English broadcaster and natural historian (1926– )

# Home Sweet Home

Many forms of life rely on *living* trees for food, shelter and reproducing.

Living trees are used for nesting, resting and as a base for hunting prey. The fruits and seeds of living trees provide sources of food.

Trees can also provide shade from extreme heat or shelter from rain.

# *Always Room for More*

Hundreds of species of fungi, moss, plants, insects and mammals can all be found living in just one single tree.

Adding a single tree to an open pasture where there were previously no birds can attract up to 80 species of birds.

Keep a green
tree in
your heart
and perhaps a
singing bird
will come.

Chinese proverb

# Nuts to Everyone

A large oak tree can drop up to

## 10,000 acorns

in one year, feeding more than 100 different species of animals. Oak trees have cycles of good and bad acorn-producing years, possibly to ensure that in a good year there will be enough acorns left over from the feast to sprout into trees.

# Out of the Decay Springs Life

As a fallen tree decays, it retains moisture that, along with the nutrients in its wood, can support soil organisms such as beetles, earthworms and other insects.

A "nurse log", a downed decaying log with soft wood tissue, is ideal for supporting several young trees during their early growth stage.

**❝**

*There are more
life forms in a handful
of forest soil than
there are people on
the planet.*

**❞**

**Peter Wohlleben,**
German forester and author (1964– )

# *There's No Place Like Home*

An amazing 80 per cent of the world's land-dwelling animals and terrestrial plants live in forests. And although tropical rainforests cover only about 6 per cent of the planet's land mass, they are home to about 50 per cent of the world's terrestrial plant and animal species.

**"**

*I never saw a*
*discontented tree.*

**"**

**John Muir**,
Scottish-American naturalist (1838–1914)

**"**

*The best friend on Earth of man is the tree. When we use the tree respectfully and economically, we have one of the greatest resources on the Earth.*

**"**

**Frank Lloyd Wright**,
Architect, writer and educator (1867–1959)

**"**

*The symbolism – and the
substantive significance – of planting a
tree has universal power
in every culture and every society
on Earth.*

**"**

**Al Gore**,
Politician and environmentalist (1948–)

# Shinrin-yoku

In Japan, studies have found that *shinrin-yoku* can improve the immune system's response, reduce stress indicators and depression, and lower glucose levels in diabetics.

*Shinrin-yoku* literally translates as "forest bathing", but in practice it involves walking in forests – no water is involved.

## *Tree Hugger*

A person who loves trees and forests is known as a dendrophile. That person could also be called another obscure term: nemophilist. Or you could simply call that person a tree hugger.

66

*Chimpanzees, gorillas and
orangutans have been living for
hundreds of thousands of years in
their forest, living fantastic lives, never
overpopulating, never destroying
the forest. I would say that they have
been in a way more successful than
us as far as being in harmony with
the environment.*

99

**Jane Goodall**,
English ethologist (1934– )

# *Same, Same but Different*

Although there are many similarities in the climates and soils of tropical rainforests around the world, each region's rainforest is unique.

The species living in an African tropical rainforest are different than those in a Central American rainforest – yet they play similar roles within their specific ecosystem.

# *Going Bats*

The kapok trees in Costa Rica's tropical rainforest are pollinated by bats – the wind then disperses the seeds.

# The Bee's Knees

Orchid bees pollinate the Brazil nut tree in the Amazon Basin, then the agouti – a large rodent native to South America – disperses the seeds.

# *Orchid Haven*

So far, scientists have recorded more than 15,000 plant species in the tropical rainforests of Borneo – and 2,500 of those species are orchids!

**66**

*At first I thought I was fighting to
save rubber trees, then I thought
I was fighting to save the
Amazon rainforest. Now I realize
I am fighting for humanity.*

**99**

**Chico Mendes**,
Brazilian environmentalist (1944–1988)

# *Amazonian Fauna*

The largest rainforest in the world, the Amazon is home to

## 427 different animal species,

such as sloths, river dolphins and anacondas. In fact, one in ten of Earth's animal species, including one in five bird species, live in the Amazon. About 100,000 invertebrate species also live in the forest.

# *Amazonian Flora*

The Amazon is home to more than

# 400 billion trees.

Although there are about 16,000 different tree species living in the Amazon, only 227 species make up about half of the total number of trees living there.

CHAPTER
**FOUR**

# Urban Trees

Discover the ecological advantages, as well as the many physical and mental health benefits, that trees provide in cities and other urban settings.

# Nature's Air Purifier

A tree's leaves and bark absorb gaseous pollutants – nitrogen oxides, ozone and carbon monoxide – and dirt, dust and soot, and release clean oxygen, perfect for animals to breathe.

A mature tree absorbs 55–110 kilograms (120–240lb) of particulate pollution annually; two medium-sized trees provide enough oxygen for one person each year.

**"**

*A nation that destroys its soils destroys itself. Forests are the lungs of our land, purifying the air and giving fresh strength to our people.*

**"**

**Franklin D. Roosevelt**,
US President (1882–1945)

## *In Europe...*

Each year, 1.3 million trees
can remove as much as

# 2,500 tonnes (2756 US tons) of pollutants

from the atmosphere.

# *In the USA...*

The United States is known for having large expanses of forests, but the trees growing in small towns and metropolitan areas alone are responsible for almost 20 per cent of the country's captured and stored carbon emissions.

# Nature's Temperature Regulator

Feeling the heat? Get out of the direct sun and head for the shade of a tree, which can reduce the temperature by as much as

## 11-25°C (20-45°F).

Not only does the shade reduce the surface temperature, but water evaporating through the leaves cools the air.

If trees are planted in the ideal positions around houses, homeowners can reduce air conditioning costs in the summer by about 30 per cent and save 20–50 per cent on heating in the winter.

Living near a large park or tract of trees could mean daytime summer air temperatures being about 5.5°C (10°F) cooler.

The best time
to plant a
tree is twenty
years ago.
The second best
time is now.

Chinese proverb

**66**

*Someone's sitting in the shade today because someone planted a tree a long time ago.*

**99**

**Warren Buffett**,
American businessman and philanthropist (1930– )

# *Better Physical Health*

Research shows that the more trees there are in an urban neighbourhood, the lower the incidence of asthma and high blood pressure.

People living in neighbourhoods with trees and plants are more likely to walk, as they may judge the distance as being less than it is.

# *Better Mental Health*

Studies have found that people living in public housing with nearby trees and grass could more effectively cope with major life issues than those living in housing surrounded by concrete.

Simply having a view of trees can provide benefits.

# *Room with a View*

Hospital patients that have a view overlooking trees recover more quickly than other patients without a similar view – probably because trees are known to help reduce stress and anxiety.

Having a view of trees from their desks made office workers more satisfied with their jobs and they showed an increased enthusiasm for work.

A tree does
not move
unless there
is wind.

Afghan proverb

# Favourite Trees in History

### Bodhi Tree:
(Bodh Gaya, India)
This sacred tree, at the Mahabodhi Temple, is thought to be a descendant from the origin fig tree under which Buddha attained enlightenment (see pages 180–1).

### Major Oak:
(Sherwood Forest, England)
It has been said that Robin Hood took refuge inside the hollow trunk of this massive 800–1,000-year-old tree.

### *Isaac Newton's Apple Tree:*
(Woolsthorpe, England)
It was an apple falling from this tree
that inspired Newton to think about the
laws of gravity. It blew down in 1820 but
has regrown from the base – and it still
produces fruit.

### *Anne Frank's Chestnut Tree:*
(Amsterdam, the Netherlands)
While in hiding during the Second World
War, Anne had views of this tree from an
attic window. It blew down in 2010.

### *September 11 Survivor Tree:*
(New York City, New York, USA)
The Callery pear tree looked dead when it
was pulled from the rubble, but it recovered
with much care and attention.

**"**

*For a tree to become tall it must grow tough roots among the rocks.*

**"**

**Friedrich Nietzsche,**
German philosopher (1844–1900)

# *Adding Value*

Having trees planted in your garden can increase your home's value.

Depending on where you live in Australia, a broad-leafed tree can add about AU$17,000.

In the United States, a large tree can add 3–15 per cent to the value of the house; in the UK, it can be up to £8,000.

**66**

*Until you dig a hole,
you plant a tree, you water
it and make it survive,
you haven't done a thing.
You are just talking.*

**99**

**Wangari Maathai**,
Kenyan social, environmental and political activist
(1940–2011)

# *Shopping Spree*

In retail areas that have street trees and green areas, consumers are

## 12 per cent more likely

to purchase goods and services.

Not only do they spend more time in these retail areas, but they will travel further to reach them.

# *More Trees, More Socializing*

Studies have found that the number of trees and their location can have a positive influence on the amount of time city residents spend outdoors in common areas; the more trees a common space have, the more local people take part in social activities.

# More Trees, Less Crime

When outdoor spaces in urban areas include natural landscaping, there is less graffiti, vandalism and littering.

Studies have also found there are 25 per cent fewer acts of domestic violence and 48 per cent fewer property crimes.

CHAPTER
**FIVE**

# Folklores and Superstitions

**From fairies and witches
to spells and songs,
here are myths, legends
and beliefs from ancient
times to modern day.**

# Bad Luck Tree

The Irish believed it was unlucky
to pass an alder tree on a journey,
and many people feared
these trees, perhaps because the pale
wood turns a deep orange colour
when cut, as if it is bleeding.

Or perhaps it's because fairies were
thought to use them to pass from
one realm to another.

# *Wand Wood*

For wind and weather magic, choose a wand made of alder wood.

Only gather branches blown down by the wind if you want the wand for wind magic. You can also choose a hazel rod to use as a wand, as well as for water-divining.

66

*Ash before oak, we're in for a soak.*
*Oak before ash, we're in for a splash.*

99

**Unknown**

**"**

*Even if I knew
that tomorrow the world
would go to pieces,
I would still plant my
apple tree.*

**"**

**Martin Luther**,
German theologian and religious reformer
(1483–1546)

# *Healing Wounds*

It was thought that burning ash would ward off evil spirits.

Ash was considered a healing tree in Britain; if you passed an ill child through a cleft opening of young ash, the child would recover.

Ash is regarded as the Tree of Life in Norse Viking mythology.

# Atlas of the Tree World

The Vikings believed that *Yggdrasil*, a huge ash tree, supported nine realms that formed the universe.

The gods lived in the centre of the ash, while humans lived in one of the realms supported by the branches.

# *The First Man and Woman*

In Norse mythology, the first man was made from the ash tree and the first woman from a rowan tree.

The rowan tree also saved the life of Thor, the god of thunder, who grabbed a tree to get back ashore after being swept away in a fast river in the Underworld.

# *Fairy Habitat*

In Britain, it was once believed that fairies lived in rowan, or mountain ash, trees because they have white flowers. It was believed that wood from these trees could protect against enchantment and witchcraft, so people hung the wood from their cattle and carried it around with them.

# If a dead tree falls, it carries with it a live one.

Kenyan proverb

# *Crying Deity*

In Japan, the sound of a crashing tree was thought to be the cry of a kodama, a deity living in the trees.

According to one account, the kodama could take on the shape of a tree, and if one were unwittingly chopped down, the woodsman would be cursed.

# Favourite Trees in Song Titles

*Don't Sit under the Apple Tree
(with Anyone Else but Me)*
by The Andrew Sisters

*Rockin' around the Christmas Tree*
by Brenda Lee

*Tie a Yellow Ribbon 'round the
Ole Oak Tree*
by Tony Orlando & Dawn

*Shaking the Tree*
by Peter Gabriel

*Fake Plastic Trees*
by Radiohead

*The Dreaming Tree*
by Dave Matthews Band

*Black Horse and the Cherry Tree*
by KT Tunstall

*Heart of Oak*
by Richard Hawley

*Coconut Tree*
by Shakira

*The Apple Tree*
by Nina Nesbitt

# *Seeking Shelter*

If a traveller shelters under
the branches of a beech
tree, no harm can come
to that person.

# Spring Cleaning

As they are among the first trees to come into leaf, birch trees are linked to the start of spring – and fertility.

A bundle of birch twigs was used to sweep away old spirits and dried leaves were used to line a baby's cot, which was thought to help a baby cast off any weakness.

# Hazel Spotty Salmon

According to Celtic lore, hazelnuts from nine hazel trees fell into a sacred pool, where the salmon in the water ate them.

These nuts contained knowledge and wisdom that were passed on to the fish, and the spots on a salmon indicate the number of nuts consumed.

## *Stopping Thieves*

If you don't want
fairies to steel your jam, stir
it with a hazel twig.

But if you want a
lucky charm, carry
a hazelnut.

If you want to be happy for a year, plant a garden; if you want to be happy for life, plant a tree.

English proverb

# Thorny Crown

Great misfortune is meant to come to anyone who destroys a hawthorn, which was once regarded as a sacred tree.

Plaited hawthorn crowns were left out for fairies to dance around and to bless the people who left them.

# *Birthplace of the Gods*

The ancient Egyptians thought that the first gods were born under an acacia tree, and the gods made decisions about life and death under this sacred tree.

# *Eternal Life*

The acorn from an oak tree is
a symbol of immortality,
and carrying one is said
to prevent illness and
ensure long life.

Perhaps that is why the
nature figure, the Green Man,
is often represented wearing a
wreath of oak leaves.

# *Tree of Life*

A mesquite tree growing in the middle of desert in Bahrain, the Tree of Life is thought to be

# 400 – 500 years old.

It's considered a miracle, as there are no other living green organisms to be found in the vast desert. Locals believe it could mark the previous location of the Garden of Eden.

# *Shaman Forests*

Groves of Scots pine in eastern Siberia were sacred to the Buriats, the Mongolian people who lived near Lake Baikal.

The groves would be approached in silence out of respect for the gods and spirits of the wood.

# American Spirits

In Sioux folklore, the canotila are forest sprites who are messengers from the spirit world and often appear in dreams. Canoti means "tree dweller" and canotila means "little tree dweller".

God gave the
giraffe a long
neck so that he
would not
have to bend the
palm tree.

Arabian proverb

CHAPTER
**SIX**

# Customs and Rituals

**Learn how trees have been celebrated and revered in ceremonies and religious rites throughout history and from around the world.**

# *Living Maypole*

As one of the first trees to come into leaf in spring, birch is often chosen for the maypole used in Beltane celebrations during the Celtic year, an event better known as May Day; sometimes a living tree is used instead.

Birch is also used in the ritual burning of Beltane fires in Scotland, which are traditionally built with birch and oak woods.

## *Floral Attire*

The blossoms from
the hawthorn tree are
used to dress up the
May Queen and May King
on May Day.

Men will only throw stones at trees laden with fruit.

French proverb

# Knock on Wood

The superstitious custom of knocking on wood for good luck goes back to the pagans, who used to tap or knock on trees to summon the protective spirits living within them.

In Turkey, a variation of this custom is to knock twice on wood and pull on an earlobe.

> **"**
>
> *A grove of giant redwood or sequoias should be kept just as we keep a great and beautiful cathedral.*
>
> **"**

**Theodore Roosevelt**,
US President (1858–1919)

**"**

*Acts of creation are ordinarily
reserved for gods and poets,
but humbler folk may circumvent this
restriction if they know how.
To plant a pine, for example,
one need be neither god or poet; one
need only own a shovel.*

**"**

**Aldo Leopard**,
American author (1887–1948)

# *From Cradle to Grave*

In Indonesia, if the babies born to the Tana Toraja tribe die before they start teething, they are buried in the hollow of a living tree.

As it grows, the tree absorbs the infant, and the members of the tribe believe this will waft away the baby's soul. Several babies can be buried in a single tree.

# Thimmamma Marrimanu

The branches of this 200-year-old banyan tree in Andhra Pradesh, India, spread out over more than 2 hectares (5 acres).

It is the local custom for a childless couple to worship at the tree's base, which they believe will lead to the arrival of a new baby the following year.

# *Carved and Scarred Trees*

The Aboriginal people of Australia traditionally carved or scarred trees for two reasons.

Trees were scarred by removing pieces of bark to use for various purposes, such as making canoes, containers, food utensils or shields.

Carved trees are a type of visual communication and are associated with spiritual purposes, such as initiation sites or to act as tombstones. Shapes include curvilinear lines, V-shaped chevrons, rare figurative images and scrolls or circles.

There are about 7,500 known scarred trees in the New South Wales territory, but less than 100 carved trees in their original sites.

# *Protecting the Future*

Trees, forests and other life forms are not inherited from your forefathers but borrowed from your unborn children.

You bear the solemn responsibility of their preservation, their enrichment.

**Native American teaching**